This book is dedicated to the memory of Virginia Robinson, Sam's Aunt Gigi (1877-1977).

Virginia spent sixty-six years of her life converting a semi-desert hillside landscape into a lush green oasis. She generously opened her home and gardens to adults and children who visited the estate to learn about plants and animals.

Upon Virginia's passing in 1977, she donated her landmark property to the people of Los Angeles County. The purpose of her generous gift was to promote the appreciation of horticulture and to inspire others to create beautiful and edible landscapes of their own.

Los Angeles County continues to use the gardens to teach elementary school children the importance and techniques of vegetable gardens through first-hand experience.

To book a guided tour: visit@robinsongardens.org
www.robinsongardens.org
(310) 550 -2087

SAM'S SUPER SALAD!

Written by Tim Lindsay and Joan Selwyn

Illustrated by Joan Selwyn

Horticultural Consultant Tim Lindsay

This was the first day of summer vacation!
Sam settled down on the couch in front of the TV.
He had dreamt of this day for months.
His plan was to sit in front of the TV, play video games,
and eat lots of jelly beans.

That night, however, Sam's dreams were shattered.
His mother announced that he would be spending the summer
at Aunt Gigi's.

"But she's an old lady and never has any jelly beans," Sam protested.
"Yes she is old," his mother replied,
"and she needs your help with her vegetable garden."

"But I hate vegetables," Sam wailed, "and she'll probably
try to make me eat them, but I won't!"

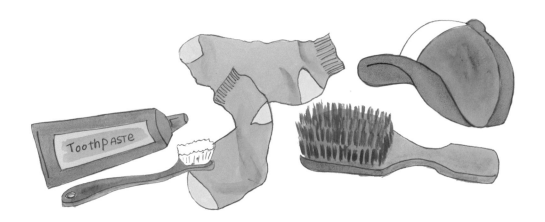

The next morning, Sam sat by his mother as they
drove to Aunt Gigi's in the country. He already missed his
friends. He looked sadly out the car window, watching the tall buildings
and busy streets passing by. He knew that this would be his worst summer ever!

When they arrived at Aunt Gigi's, Sam pleaded,
"Don't leave me Mom. I don't want to help in a vegetable garden."

Aunt Gigi ran out to greet them. She gave Sam such a big hug
that he could not be mad anymore.

As Sam's mother drove away, she smiled. She knew that Sam
was going to enjoy his summer with Aunt Gigi.

"I'll see you in two months," she called out to Sam.

Aunt Gigi said, "Come into the house. I've made us lunch."
" I hope it's a juicy cheeseburger with fries," thought Sam.

But no. It was a giant salad, made of lettuce, spinach, kale, tomatoes, carrots, cucumbers, and yellow peppers.

"Yuck, I hate vegetables," thought Sam.

"I've grown all the vegetables for the salad in my garden," said Aunt Gigi.
"Try it, you might like it."
"I don't think so," Sam thought, but he took a small bite, and then another.

It really wasn't as bad as he expected.

After lunch, Aunt Gigi took Sam to see her vegetable garden.
He had only seen vegetables in a grocery store."It's pretty nice," he said,
looking at all the colorful fruits and vegetables. He recognized the tomatoes.
Aunt Gigi said, "Tomatoes have seeds in them and are actually a fruit
and not a vegetable".

Then she pointed to large heads of lettuce and some spinach and said,
"These have no seeds and are called vegetables."

Sam then spotted some ferny green leaves growing out of the ground.
"What is this ?" he asked. "Those are carrots," Aunt Gigi said.

"But I don't see any carrots," Sam said.
Aunt Gigi smiled, "That is because carrots grow underground.
Some vegetables grow up, and some grow down, and some
grow along the ground."

They reached a section of the garden where there was just bare ground. "What's planted here?" Sam asked. "Nothing yet,"Aunt Gigi answered. "This is where I need your help. OK?"

"Sure," Sam replied, seeing his dream of TV and video games and jelly beans fade even further away.

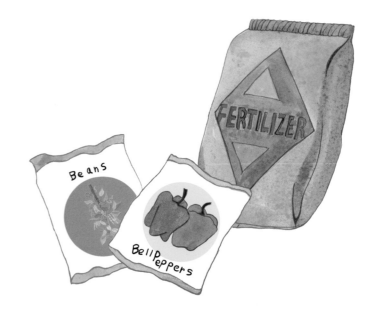

Aunt Gigi woke Sam early the next morning. "After breakfast, we will begin our work," she said. He ate some cereal with berries, and then Aunt Gigi handed him a shovel and said, "The first thing we do is make the soil ready for the seeds; so dig as deep as you can and turn the soil over."

"This is hard work," Sam thought, but soon he finished.

Aunt Gigi said," Next take the rake and make the ground smooth." "Oh no, another job Sam moaned to himself, but soon he finished that job too.

"Now the ground is ready for the seeds, "expalined Aunt Gigi.
"Take your finger and draw a straight line in the dirt." Sam did this. It was fun!

He held out his hand, and she poured some little grey things into his palm.
She said,"These are carrot seeds. Poke holes in the line you drew and put
a seed in each one."Sam did this, and it was fun, too. "Now cover them with
a little bit of soil, and sprinkle them with water." said Aunt Gigi with a smile.

Each day, they waited for the seeds to come up. Sam helped weed the garden, gather vegetables, and pick lemons from the lemon tree and apples from the apple tree.

He helped make icy cold lemonade and delicious apple pies.

"This," Sam thought, "is almost as much fun as playing video games and eating jelly beans."

One morning, Sam asked Aunt Gigi if the seeds had sprouted.
"Not yet," she answered. "So today we'll plant some beets and
water the seeds."

After two weeks, Aunt Gigi finally answered, "YES! the carrot
seeds have sprouted." Sam rushed into the garden and saw tiny
green ferny leaves poking just above the soil. He picked up the
watering can and watered all the tiny seedlings.

He could hardly wait to taste those crunchy carrots!

After breakfast the next day, he ran into the garden and couldn't believe what he saw. Many of the leaves on the plants had been eaten! "What happened?" he asked Aunt Gigi.

"Snails," she replied, "But we can catch them and then plant the seeds again."

So Sam and Aunt Gigi caught many snails and planted more seeds.

Sam was spending almost all day in the garden pulling weeds, watering the plants that were growing taller, and watching the butterflies and hummingbirds flying from plant to plant and tree to tree.

He watched the bees gathering nectar and thought about what Aunt Gigi had told him. As bees gather nectar from flowers, the pollen sticks to them. When they visit other flowers, they bring the pollen with them. This helps the flowers make seeds and delicious fruit to eat.

"I really like to garden," Sam thought. "I'll ask Aunt Gigi if
I can have a garden in the city."

"It's as easy to have a garden in the city as it is to have one in the
country, "she told Sam. "Just like people, vegetables need sun, water
and fresh air. You find the sunniest spot to start your garden,
whether it is in a window box, an empty lot, or even in an old tire.
All you need is soil, sun and, water."

"What should I grow? "asked Sam.
"How about all the vegetables that make a good salad?"
suggested Aunt Gigi.

"I like salad almost as much as jelly beans,"
Sam said, surprising himself.

Aunt Gigi explained, "In an apartment you don't have a yard full of soil in which to plant. You have to get a planter box and fill it with about three inches of pebbles. Then you add enough soil, or planter mix, and pat it down with your hands."

"Why do you need the pebbles?" Sam asked.
Aunt Gigi explained, "The pebbles help to drain away the water if the soil is too wet. Too much water isn't good for the roots."

Aunt Gigi continued, "Next you make some rows with your fingers and then some holes, just like you did in the garden. You put a seed in each hole, cover it with a little soil, and water the seeds whenever the soil gets dry to the touch. Now won't that be easy?"

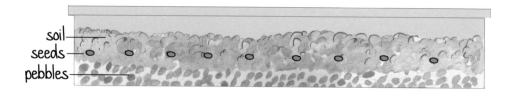

soil
seeds
pebbles

Summer had been more fun than Sam could have imagined.
Soon it was time to go back to the city. "Before you go," Aunt Gigi said,
" let's invite your friends and have a harvest picnic. They can help you
pick the vegetables you planted, and make a super salad that we can all enjoy."

A few days later, Sam's friends arrived from the city. They all picked
vegetables. They washed and cut the vegetables and prepared a gigantic salad.
Aunt Gigi made pitchers of lemonade, and apple and lemon pies.

As they sat around the table in the garden, Sam looked
at his friends and they gave each other a big "thumbs up."

Sam said, "Thanks, Aunt Gigi. Now we know how to turn our city
into one huge garden."

AND THEY DID!

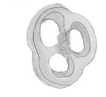

SAM'S SUPER SALAD!
Recipe

Sam's Super Salad is easy to make with your parents. It is delicious and healthy.

INGREDIENTS
Wash all vegetables under tap water.
2 cups of grated carrots
1 tomato cut into small pieces
1/2 of a yellow pepper cut into strips
4 cups of chopped spinach and romaine lettuce leaves
1 bunch kale, stemmed and finely chopped

BALSAMIC VINAIGRETTE DRESSING
3 tablespoons balsamic vinegar
1 tablespoon Dijon mustard
2 tablespoons fresh lemon juice
1 garlic clove, minced
1/2 cup of olive oil

Whisk first four ingredients in a medium size bowl.
Gradually stir in oil. Add a pinch of salt and pepper.
Let stand at room temperature for 15 minutes; rewhisk before using.
Add dressing to salad and toss.

Some fun stuff to add to your salad - Goldfish crackers, bits of bacon, sunflower seeds, cheese, or nuts